Schwerpunktthema **Abitur Englisch**

East Is East
A Film Study

Cornelsen

East Is East A Film Study

von Sabine Struß

Verlagsredaktion
Dr. Marion Kiffe

Layoutkonzept
Annika Preyhs für Buchgestaltung+, Berlin

Technische Umsetzung
krauß-verlagsservice, Niederschönenfeld

Umschlaggestaltung
orangerie-grafikdesign

Umschlagfoto
© Shutterstock / Yayakumar

www.cornelsen.de

1. Auflage, 1. Druck 2016

Alle Drucke dieser Auflage sind inhaltlich unverändert und können im Unterricht nebeneinander verwendet werden.

Druck: H. Heenemann, Berlin

ISBN 978-3-06-035239-5

PEFC
PEFC/04-31-1156

PEFC zertifiziert
Dieses Produkt stammt aus nachhaltig bewirtschafteten Wäldern und kontrollierten Quellen.

www.pefc.de

PART I INTRODUCTION

Dear student,
East Is East is a film that is difficult to categorize – from one scene to the next, viewers experience different emotions as the film swings from hilarity to heartbreak and back again. It is as much a tragedy as a comedy and evokes strong sympathy for the various characters, leaving viewers on a feel-good high by the end of the movie.

The film opens with the Khan children taking part in a Catholic procession. In order to avoid being seen by their strict Pakistani father George, they take a detour through the back streets. The multicultural setting and the lively atmosphere are heightened by the catchy music and immediately cast a spell on us as viewers. Simultaneously, we are given an idea of the conflicts that might lie ahead.

George Khan runs a fish and chip shop in Salford and unquestionably is the head of the family. His English wife Ella is torn between meeting her husband's expectations, holding the family together and maintaining her British identity. However, their six children each find their own way of dealing with the family's problems: Nazir refuses an arranged marriage to a Pakistani woman and moves in with his partner. Sajid, the youngest son, mostly searches for hiding places even if this is only in his oversized parka. Meenah, the only daughter, prefers playing football in the street to acting like a typical girl. Tariq, Abdul and Saleem all try to find their own ways of avoiding or coping with their father's strict Pakistani values, while the peace-loving Maneer seems to be happy to go along with anything.

Negative aspects of family life such as George's rough behaviour and the family's fierce arguments are set side by side with tender or humorous scenes. This constant juxtaposition of elements keeps the movie lively and allows each viewer to find their favourite themes within it. Thus, the microcosm of a multicultural family in a northern English town in the 1970s reveals several universal themes, such as growing up between two cultures, questions of identity and loyalty, friendship, racism, and religious rites and traditions. The complexity of these aspects combined with clever film-making techniques definitely make the film worth watching in class.

This booklet provides you with many tasks that will help you to gain a deeper understanding of the film. You might wish to do some pre-viewing tasks before watching the full movie and then continue with while-viewing tasks. Both the while-viewing and the post-viewing section offer a large choice of tasks and ideas that include various themes from the film and help you to train important skills such as viewing, listening, reading, writing, speaking, and mediation. Language help or tips are often included next to tasks. The FILM STUDIES EXTRA section at the end gives an overview of cinematic devices and provides useful phrases and expressions which you can use to increase your vocabulary.

Sabine Struß

PART II INFORMATION ABOUT THE FILM

1 EAST IS EAST

Directed by Damien O'Donnell
Play and Screenplay Ayub Khan-Din
Starring Om Puri
Linda Bassett

2 THE PLOT

East Is East is set in the suburb of Salford in Manchester in the 1970s, a time when British politician Enoch Powell's warnings against immigration to Britain resounded through the country (cf. p. 21). The film is about the Khan family; a mixed-race family headed by George, a Pakistani immigrant who came to the UK 25 years ago, his wife Ella, a white Roman Catholic woman, and their seven children.

Even after 25 years in the UK George has not integrated fully into British society and is determined that his seven children will follow Islamic traditions. However, his eldest son, Nazir, refuses to agree to an arranged marriage with a Pakistani woman and runs away from home. As a result, George declares him dead. In order to assert his authority in the family and force his children to accept traditional Muslim values, he arranges marriages for his next two sons, Tariq and Abdul, to two Pakistani sisters. Even though the family accept the decision at first, George's strict methods of raising children and his traditional mindset lead to conflicts within the family.

George tries hard to defend his position as head of the family and uphold traditional Muslim customs within the family. He and Ella often argue about questions of power and identity within the family. In contrast to George, the children are well integrated into the community and (partly secretly) reject their father's traditional rules on religion, food, dress and life in general. When the plans for Tariq and Abdul's arranged marriages are discovered, Ella and George quarrel about the children's upbringing and this culminates in George beating Ella up. The children look to their eldest brother for support, but not even Nazir, who lives in London and turns out to be gay, dares to revolt openly against his father.

A few days later, the Shah family and the brides-to-be arrive for a visit. A series of comic and embarrassing incidents ensue, and the visit ends in disaster. The Shahs leave, insulted, and Tariq and Abdul's engagements are broken off. Only then do Ella and her sons stand up to George, which finally forces him to rethink the family structure.

3 MAIN CHARACTERS

The Khans				Others	
George Khan	father	**Ella Khan**	mother	**Annie**	neighbour
Nazir	first son	**Abdul**	second son	**Mr Moorhouse**	neighbour
Tariq	third son	**Saleem**	fourth son	**Stella**	Mr Moorhouse's granddaughter
Maneer	fifth son	**Meenah**	daughter		
Sajid	sixth son			**Peggy**	Stella's friend

4 SCENE INDEX

Time	Characters/Action
0:00:00 – 0:02:47	**Street Parade**
	The Khan children are taking part in a Catholic procession. Ella is warned by her friend Annie that George is approaching and Ella advises her children to take an alternate route so that George will not see them.
0:02:48 – 0:0:23	**Proud Father**
	At the Khans' home the family is preparing for Nazir's wedding. Nazir is led downstairs by George and the family drives to the church hall in a colourfully decorated van, watched by neighbours. In the church hall the celebratory atmosphere of the wedding ceremony is interrupted when Nazir suddenly runs away. Back home, George removes Nazir's picture from the wall with the family portraits.
0:09:24 – 0:09:59	**Cod & Two Wives**
	In the mosque, George and the mullah deplore Nazir's behaviour. Six months later, the scene shows the children playing in the street while Ella and Annie work in the chip shop. A Catholic priest comes to collect roses and shamrocks for the procession. George enters listening to the news on his portable radio and makes fun of the priest collecting flowers. In the courtyard, Tariq and Stella embrace and kiss while Stella's friend Peggy looks on. In the chip shop George hears bad news from Pakistan and wonders about the fate of his first wife. Ella refuses to let her come over to Britain and George stands at the window smoking and watching his children play in the street. When the van arrives to take everyone to the mosque, the children aren't ready. Maneer interrupts Tariq and Stella kissing in the courtyard. Stella says to Peggy that Tariq is 'the only bit of happiness' she has. Sajid has to be pulled out from under the bed by George. In the mosque, apart from Maneer, all the Khan children are more or less bored during the Koran lesson. Abdul is shown at his workplace where he looks at a poster of a nude woman in a workmate's locker and then stumbles across a workmate's stag party.

Time	Characters/Action
0:15:11 – 0:23:05	**I'll Fix Him**
	The boys are having a peeing contest in the mosque yard, when the mullah discovers that Sajid is not circumcized. At the Khan's home the mullah tells George, who blames his wife for the oversight. When Annie takes a look and verifies the accusation, Sajid escapes to the coal shed in the back garden. The Khan children are cleaning up the chip shop. Saleem draws a penis, and the children wonder about the significance of the foreskin. They are surprised when Maneer says he believes that it does not influence feeling during sex. In the backyard George and Ella argue about the religious necessity of circumcision, about to whom the house belongs and about who is boss. A neighbour's complaint is shouted down by Annie. The family attempt to make Sajid leave the coal shed. Sajid is eventually circumcized. After the operation, when George and Ella pick up Sajid from the hospital, George is suspicious of the (Indian?) doctor. He gives Sajid a watch with his name in Arabic. Back home the Khan children are having a bacon-and-sausage feast while on TV Enoch Powell speaks against immigrants. Earnest asks after Sajid. When George enters the room carrying Sajid in his arms, the others try to get rid of the smell of bacon. Sajid is put on the sofa in the parlour. Meenah tears a drawing of a penis in half to tease him. Later in the chip shop courtyard Meenah dances to traditional Indian music with her broom while Maneer cuts up fish. Tariq and Saleem watch and smoke. Annie is on her way to the Khans' house.
0:23:06 – 0:27:07	**A Good Mother**
	Ella is looking after Sajid and asks Annie if she is a good mother. In the mosque the mullah tells George about Mr Shah, who has two girls ready to be married. George agrees to meet him and discuss marrying Abdul and Tariq off to Mr Shah's daughters. At home George shows Ella an old barber's chair, which he has bought for her. While she is lying back in it he proposes a trip to Bradford to see a film, which makes Ella slightly suspicious.
0:27:08 – 0:35:24	**Your Daughters Are My Daughters**
	At home Sajid is talking to Earnest and waiting to go to Bradford. The family gets ready to leave and George takes Tariq's and Abdul's photos from the wall with him. During the trip in the van George talks about his arrival in England in 1937. A town sign can be seen on which Bradford has been changed into 'Bradistan'. In Bradford the influence of the Pakistani community can be seen and Ella explicitly refuses to move to Bradford. In the friend's house in Bradford men and boys are gathered in the living room. George expresses unhappiness that his sons do not speak Urdu. When Mr Shah arrives with the mullah the boys are told to leave. Ella and Meenah sit in the kitchen with a friend's English wife and look at photos of their daughter, who is married and lives in Pakistan. The mother cries. A knock on the wall signals it is time for the men's tea. In the living room photos of Tariq and Abdul and of Mr Shah's daughters are passed around. Mr Shah embarrasses George by mentioning his 'six' sons. George seems shocked by the pictures of the girls, but then, to everyone's relief, he agrees and the engagement is fixed.

Time	Characters/Action
0:35:25 – 0:41:57	**Night on the Town**
	In Bradford, the Khan family go to a cinema which is owned by a relative. They interrupt a film viewing and are granted a viewing of another Asian film of their choice. At home Tariq and Abdul sneak out of their bedroom to the disco. It is Abdul's first time and he is very curious. At the club, Tariq is known as Tony, Abdul is only admitted when 'Tony' explains he is his brother and Abdul calls himself Arthur. Tony is popular with the girls; Stella and Peggy have to fight their way to him. Peggy tries to kiss Abdul, who is obviously out of his depth.
0:41:58 – 0:45:03	**A Right to Know**
	At night Ella and George are making love in their bedroom. Sajid is pushed away from the pee-bucket in the boys' room by his drunk brothers returning from the disco and is told to pee in their parents' bucket. After being detected he runs out of the room and catches his anorak string in the door. He overhears George telling Ella about the engagement. Ella wants George to tell their sons, but he is not cooperative and warns Ella not to meddle in his business.
0:45:04 – 0:51:38	**Say Nothing**
	The next morning George warns Ella to keep quiet. Ella has received a parcel with a new hat from Nazir and calls the kids down to breakfast (tea and biscuits). She starts talking to Abdul but thinks better of it. George buys wedding apparel for his sons at an Asian market, including watches with Arabic inscriptions of their names. In the street Stella asks after Tariq and Peggy tries to flirt with Saleem. Stella's grand-father (Mr Moorhouse) is actively supporting Powell's call for the repatriation of immigrants. Tariq and Stella are snogging and dismiss Peggy, who feels insulted when told to go away but is subsequently pacified by the offer of a week's free chips and a Coke. George approaches in a bad mood and the girls hide from him. George is busy criticizing his sons for not looking smart and traditional when he is interrupted by Stella and Peggy crying for help as they are accosted by a large Dalmatian.
0:51:39 – 0:59:66	**What Engagement?**
	Ella and her children are walking through heavy rain to secretly phone Nazir from a phone box while George sits at home. The next day, the children play football in the street. Earnest asks Meenah to play and she aims at an Enoch Powell poster and breaks the window behind it. She runs away with a triumphant smile as Earnest's grandfather looks through the hole, furious. At home Sajid is spying on one of his brothers to compare his penis to Saleem's drawing when Meenah sees him and calls him a pervert. A fight starts, which Sajid can only escape by revealing what he knows about the secret engagement. In the parents' bedroom, Tariq searches for hints at the engagement and opens his father's trunk. He drags everything out and stamps on the watches while the others watch aghast. Tariq wrongly accuses Maneer of having known about the engagement and when they hear George coming they run away, only Maneer stays and tries to tidy up. George wants to know who did it and he beats Maneer for not telling him. George drags Maneer out of the house, takes him to Ella in the chip shop and, when she tries to protect Maneer, beats her up as well. Maneer looks on from behind the blurred coloured strips of the curtain; Sajid watches fearfully from outside.

Time	Characters/Action
0:59:66 – 1:05:30	**Enough's Enough**
	Ella and the kids are watching TV together ('This crowded planet – our home'). George is alone in another room. Saleem asks for more money for his sculpture and promises to bring the finished product on Sunday. Ella announces the Shahs' visit on Sunday: the whole family must attend, including Saleem. Tariq leaves the room in anger. Tariq decides to leave the family, Abdul stays behind and does as his father says; Saleem and Meenah join Tariq (as do Stella and Peggy, who follow them with packed suitcases).
1:05:31 – 1:08:50	**You'll Make Things Worse**
	They travel to Eccles by bus, where Nazir works as a milliner. They discover that Nazir is gay and decide not to stay. Nazir and his boyfriend drive them all home in their Rolls Royce. Ella prevents a showdown between Nazir and George, and sends Nazir and his boyfriend away with Sajid running behind the car and George looking on pensively. George fastens a lock to his trunk and makes sure it is firmly secured.
1:08:51– 1:13:33	**Show Me Respect**
	The family are watching a news item on the war in East Pakistan. George tells them to turn off the TV, describes the dress code for Sunday and warns his family to behave and show respect for the Shahs. In a pub Abdul is drinking a pint on his own because he's getting married the next day. He considers it his stag night as he tells a few workmates, who are surprised to see him there. In the chip shop courtyard George is cutting up fish and Tariq is trying to make him see his point of view. Tariq explains that he wants to choose his own wife. George threatens him with the fish knife when Tariq reminds him that he himself married an English woman. Tariq promises to do as he is told and when his father lowers the knife, Tariq runs off saying that he will marry a Pakistani woman first and then an English woman of his own choice, just as George did.
1:13:34 – 1:20:25	**Mr Shah's Daughters**
	The Shahs arrive at the Khans' house. Sajid nearly gets hit by their car and gives them the finger before he realizes who they are. He runs inside shouting 'The Pakis are here!' The neighbours watch the arrival curiously. When Earnest greets Mr Shah 'Salamaleikum', Mr Shah seems annoyed and tells him to 'bugger off'. The families greet each other and there is a first viewing of the prospective brides and grooms followed by some polite conversation. Annie joins them and outside there is some commotion.
1:20:26 – 1:23:45	**The Sculpture**
	Saleem comes in with his 'sculpture', which is a reproduction of female genitals made from rubber. After a scuffle in the hall, the sculpture falls into Mrs Shah's lap. The Shahs leave in disgust, with Ella telling them to 'piss off'. The Dalmatian (encouraged by Ella) jumps on Mrs Shah before she can get in the car.

Time	Characters/Action
1:23:46 – 1:29:49	**I Know What's Best**
	George is furious and calls Ella a 'bastard bitch'. Ella accuses him of being ashamed of her and their children, then he beats her. Abdul tries to separate them and in the process, the hood of Sajid's parka comes off. Sajid runs out. Ella tells George to leave. As he leaves the house, Earnest greets him in Arabic, George greets him back glumly. After the argument, Ella takes George's side and tells the kids that he's still their father. Abdul tries to coax Sajid out of the coal shed in the backyard; they decide to throw the parka hood away. Ella visits George in the chip shop and makes tea for him. In the street Sajid (at last without his parka) shows Earnest Saleem's sculpture; there is again a scuffle. Peggy is angry and reminds Seelem of his promise not to show anyone. Playful shouting can be heard.
1:30:00 – 1:32:50	**End Credits**

PART III SHORT TASKS ON THE FILM

Before watching the film, you might wish to consider these tasks:

1 Name films that deal with the clash between cultures. Describe your reaction to them.

2 In what way might different ethnic backgrounds of parents affect family life and the upbringing of children? Collect ideas.

3 Describe how children's plans for the future may be different from their parents' hopes or expectations.

The following tasks might be interesting to consider while viewing the film:

4 Describe the attitude towards the two cultures shown in the film.

5 Examine the role of music in the film.

6 Describe the role the setting plays. Think of the street where the Khans live, the house interior, Bradford, etc.

7 Describe how the different characters in the film express emotions.

8 Describe how the film portrays the long-standing relationship between a Pakistani husband and his British wife.

9 Describe the function of the characters outside the Khan family. Which of these characters is most memorable to you? Why?

After watching the film, you could consider these questions:

10 The film deals with events that took place about three decades before its production and release. What do you think made it so successful? What would be different if it was about today's multicultural Britain?

11 Do you think *East Is East* is a comedy? Which scenes do you consider humorous and which ones seem to belong to a different genre altogether?

12 The film deals not only with a clash of cultures, but also with class distinctions. Which scenes might this refer to and how is this class distinction made apparent by filming techniques?

13 How does the film deal with gender? Consider the two women in the Khan family as well as the woman they visit in Bradford whose daughter married a Pakistani man.

PART IV PRE-VIEWING ACTIVITIES

1 WHAT TO EXPECT? – A THINK-PAIR-SHARE ACTIVITY

family life
Pakistan Muslim
religion
old-fashioned

A 00:21:43

B 00:02:12

C 00:54:47

- typical of childhood in 70s
- school uniforms
- soccer in the street

D 00:09:10

wedding ceremony
India
no complete happiness
arranged marriage

E 01:24:53

1 **Think:** Choose one still and write down five words that spontaneously come to your mind in response to it.

____

____

____

____

____

____

____

2 **Pair:** Present your results to a partner, then write down what the characters might be saying.

3 **Share:** Present your results. In class, discuss what the film might be about.

2 A WORDLE

The wordle below consists of topics that play an important role in the film *East Is East*.

1 Imagine a possible storyline of a film that involves as many of the topics from the wordle as possible.

a WRITING Write a short text to describe your storyline (about 150 words).

b SPEAKING Get together in groups of four and read out your texts to each other. Compare the various ideas and discuss whether you would like to watch the film. Why or why not?

3 ASIAN IMMIGRATION TO THE UK – RESEARCH & PRESENTATION

1 In class, collect topics to do with Asian immigration to Britain that you would like to know more about. Make sure to include the history of the British Empire and the Commonwealth as well.

2 Form groups and divide the topics up among your groups.

3 Brainstorm questions that you can use as guidelines for your research on your topic.

4 Carry out your research. The website www.bbc.co.uk may offer helpful information. Collect information, and then structure it.

5 Prepare some written or digital materials to accompany your presenta-tion (e. g. flip chart, poster, digital presentation tool, hand-outs, …).

6 Practise your presentation with your group members.

7 SPEAKING Give your presentation and ask your audience for feedback.

Criteria for evaluating presentations

	well done (comments)	needs some work (comments/advice)
content: – quality of information – structure		
media: – variety – handling – function		
language: – fluency – variety of vocabulary		
body language: – gestures – facial expression		
interaction with the audience		

PART IV WHILE-VIEWING ACTIVITIES

1 MEMORABLE QUOTES – GETTING THE GIST

1 COMPREHENSION + ANALYSIS Describe the context of each scene below and explain its function in the film.

1	George: '... when I come this country, I have no luggage. Today what I got?' Meenah: 'You got a chip shop, Dad.' George: 'Right. Own bloody business, see.'	
2	George: 'Tickle-tackle all gone?' Doctor: 'Circumcision was absolutely fine.' George: 'You Indian?' Ella: 'George!' George: 'Bastard Indian.'	
3	Tariq: [*Watching* Enoch *Powell speaking on TV*] 'We should have a whip-round and get Dad repatriated.'	
4	Bouncer: 'All right, Tony, how ya goin' mate?' Tariq: 'All right, Bazza?' Bouncer: 'Yeah, good to see ya. All right, in ya go.' Tariq: 'Nice, mate.' Bouncer: [*to Abdul*] 'Where do you think you're going, smiler?' Tariq: 'This is our kid, erm ...' Abdul: 'Arthur, me name's Arthur.'	
5	Ella: 'But I'll tell you one thing, she'll find it hard serving fish and chips dressed in bedsheets.'	

6	Stella: 'Let's elope. That's soooo romantic.' Tariq: 'We can't. I'm eloping on me own.'	
7	Stella: 'See. You let one of 'em in, and the whole fuckin' tribe turns up.'	
8	Meenah: 'Have you seen the state of them two? One of 'em's got a moustache like Dad.' Ella: 'Kids eh. Were your two like that, Mrs. Shah?' Mrs Shah: 'No.'	
9	Mrs Shah: 'I believe in strict discipline. Especially in a non-Pakistani environment.'	
10	Mrs Shah: 'I will never allow my daughters to marry into this jungly family of half-breeds.' Ella: 'Well they may be half-bred, but at least they're not friggin' inbred like those two monstrosities.'	
11	Sajid: 'Mum! Mum! The Pakis are here!'	
12	Mark: 'Gunga Din! Drinking the white man's brew!' Workmate: 'What are you doing here, Abdul?' Abdul: 'It's me stag night. I'm gettin' married.' Mark: 'Who to?' Abdul: 'Dunno. Me dad hasn't bothered introducing us yet.'	

2 Outline crucial topics of the film as they are presented in the quotes. Pay special attention to intercultural as well as intracultural aspects.

2 THE OPENING SEQUENCE

1 Before watching: What do you expect to be shown in the first three minutes of a film? Make notes.

2 VIEWING Watch the beginning of *East Is East* (0:00:00 – 0:02:56).
  a Compare the beginning of the movie with your notes: which of your expectations were met, which weren't?
  b The following is a list of statements about opening sequences of movies. Decide which of them are true for *East Is East*:
    A Establishing shots are used to set the scene and inform the audience about where the story takes place.
    B The music in the opening scene is quiet and slow-paced, gradually putting the viewers in the right mood.
    C A narrator gives background information.
    D You get a sense of the genre and the pace of the movie.
    E Flashbacks provide the necessary background information.
    F An action scene or a chase scene catches the audience's attention and makes them want to see what is going to happen.
    G There is an unconventional opening, i.e. no credits, no establishing shots or no introduction of the main characters.

3 Summarize what we learn about the setting, the characters, the storyline and the genre.

4 ANALYSIS Analyse what cinematic devices are employed to establish the characters and the genre and to make the audience curious about how the story will continue. Focus on the atmosphere as well.

5 SPEAKING Choose either task a or b.
  a Choose two stills from the first two minutes of the film (cf. p. 20) and analyse them with regard to camera range, camera angle and cinematic devices employed (cf. FILM STUDIES EXTRA pp. 47 ff.). Make notes about each still, then compare your results in a double circle or milling around activity.
  b Divide the class into three groups. Each group deals with one still: Analyse it with regard to camera range, camera angle and cinematic devices (cf. FILM STUDIES EXTRA pp. 47 ff.). Form new groups of at least three members making sure that each still is represented in each group. Present your results to each other.

TIP

The FILM STUDIES EXTRA section (cf. pp. 47 ff.) explains important film vocabulary and contains many useful phrases and expressions that you can use for your analysis.

A 00:01:56

B 00:02:14

C 00:02:08

3 'I SEE THE RIVER TIBER FOAMING WITH MUCH BLOOD' – ANALYSING A SPEECH

Read the following speech, which was given by Enoch Powell, Member of Parliament for the Conservative Party, on 20 April 1968.

In 15 or 20 years, on present trends, there will be in this country three and a half million Commonwealth immigrants and their descendants. That is not my figure. That is the official figure given to parliament by the spokesman of the Registrar General's Office. There is no comparable official figure for the year 2000, but it must be in the region of five to seven million, approximately one-tenth of the whole population, and approaching that of Greater London. Of course, it will not be evenly distributed from Margate to Aberystwyth and from Penzance to Aberdeen. Whole areas, towns and parts of towns across England will be occupied by sections of the immigrant and immigrant-descended population.

As time goes on, the proportion of this total who are immigrant descendants, those born in England, who arrived here by exactly the same route as the rest of us, will rapidly increase. Already by 1985 the native-born would constitute the majority. It is this fact which creates the extreme urgency of action now, of just that kind of action which is hardest for politicians to take, action where the difficulties lie in the present but the evils to be prevented or minimized lie several parliaments ahead.

The natural and rational first question with a nation confronted by such a prospect is to ask: 'How can its dimensions he reduced?' Granted it be not wholly preventable, can it be limited, bearing in mind that numbers are of the essence: the significance and consequences of an alien element introduced into a country or population are profoundly different according to whether that element is 1 per cent or 10 per cent. The answers to the simple and rational question are equally simple and rational: by stopping, or virtually stopping, further inflow, and by promoting the maximum outflow. Both answers are part of the official policy of the Conservative Party.

It almost passes belief that at this moment 20 or 30 additional immigrant children are arriving from overseas in Wolverhampton alone every week – and that means 15 or 20 additional families a decade or two hence. Those whom the gods wish to destroy, they first make mad. We must be mad, literally mad, as a nation to be permitting the annual inflow of some 50,000 dependants, who are for the most part the material of the future growth of the immigrant-descended population. It is like watching a nation busily engaged in heaping up its own funeral pyre. [...]

2 *descendant* Nachkomme

7 *evenly distributed* gleichmäßig verteilt

11 *proportion* Anteil

19 *granted it be not preventable* if we accept that it cannot be prevented

20 *be of the essence* be important, crucial

27 *it almost passes belief* it is nearly unbelievable

29 *hence* from now

34 *heaping up its own funeral pyre* seinen eigenen Scheiterhaufen errichten

In these circumstances nothing will suffice but that the total inflow for settlement should be reduced at once to negligible proportions, and that the necessary legislative and administrative measures be taken without delay. [...]

As I look ahead, I am filled with foreboding; like the Roman, I seem to see 'the River Tiber foaming with much blood'. That tragic and intractable phenomenon which we watch with horror on the other side of the Atlantic but which there is interwoven with the history and existence of the States itself, is coming upon us here by our own volition and our own neglect. Indeed, it has all but come. In numerical terms, it will be of American proportions long before the end of the century. Only resolute and urgent action will avert it even now. Whether there will be the public will to demand and obtain that action, I do not know. All I know is that to see, and not to speak, would be the great betrayal.

From: Enoch Powell, Address to the General Meeting of the West Midlands Area Conservative Political Centre, 20 April 1968

36 *negligible* [ˈ – – – –] of little importance

39 *foreboding* feeling that sth. bad is going to happen

40 *'River Tiber ...'* reference to Virgil's Aneid, in which he predicts bloody battles between Troy and Rome before Rome would rise again as a multi-ethnic city

43 *volition* will, decision

44 *all but* in fact, already

46 *avert sth.* prevent sth.

1 COMPREHENSION Decide whether the following statements are true or false, according to the speaker.
  a In 1968, Powell estimates that in the year 2000 there will be about 10 million Commonwealth immigrants in the UK.
  b Most immigrants will be living in Greater London.
  c The Conservatives' official policy is to stop immigrants coming to the UK and to encourage them to go back to their countries of origin.
  d Powell finds it incredible that every week 20 to 30 immigrant children arrive in the UK on their own.
  e Powell considers it madness that nothing is being done to prevent immigrants from arriving in the UK.

2 ANALYSIS Explain what Powell means by a 'tragic and intractable phenomenon' (l. 40).

3 ANALYSIS Analyse the speaker's use of language and explain in what way Powell uses stylistic devices to emphasize his point.

4 WRITING Comment on Powell's ideas. You might take into consideration both the history of the United States as a nation of immigrants and migration into Europe in the 21st century.

4 THE MAIN CHARACTERS – TANDEM PRESENTATIONS

1 ANALYSIS Divide the class into two groups. Students in group A focus on Ella, those in group B on George. While watching the film, make notes for a description of your character. Be careful to consider the following aspects:
- facts, family background and appearance
- the character's behaviour and interaction with others
- their attitudes, beliefs, values and feelings.

2 Prepare a short oral presentation about your character.

3 SPEAKING Pair up with a partner from the other group. Each of you give a presentation on your character.

4 After the presentations, tick the three adjectives in the box below that describe your partner's character best. Discuss your choices with your partner (cf. the useful vocabulary at the bottom of the page).

Character: ____________________

G	aggressive		amiable	G	authoritarian		caring
	concerned	G	conservative	G	determined	G	dominant
	good-hearted		middle-class		protective	G	rude
	scared	G	self-centred		sensitive		subservient
G	torn	G	traditional	G	uneducated		vulgar
	weak		well-mannered		well-meaning		

Useful vocabulary:

Stating your opinion	**Agreeing**	**Disagreeing**
Well, I'd say ... If you ask me ... It seems to me that ... I think/feel/believe ... First of all ... / To start with ...	I quite agree. That's true/right. / That's just it. Exactly!/Precisely!/Certainly!/Definitely! You're quite right. I think so too. You've got a good point there. Yes, indeed.	I'm not so sure, really. Do you really think so? Well, that's one way of looking at it, but ... I'm not convinced that ... Well, I have my doubts about that.

5 GEORGE KHAN

5.1 UNDERSTANDING GEORGE'S BEHAVIOUR

1 VIEWING Watch the following two sequences and tick the sentence that summarizes the scene best.

a 0:24:29 – 0:25:36 04:06 - 05.31

A George meets the mullah to arrange the marriages of two of his sons.

B George is worried about his reputation as a good Pakistani.

C George wants his sons to become full members of the Muslim community.

b 0:50:43 – 0:51:32

A George thinks his sons aren't working properly in the backyard.

B George tells them to go and help their mother.

C George is annoyed about his sons' clothes and hairdo.

2 Explain George's behaviour. What might be his underlying motifs, fears, hopes, etc.?

3 Discuss in what way the two stills below represent the different facets of George's personality.

A 00:51:04

B 00:36:08

5.2 OM PURI'S THOUGHTS ON GEORGE

Om Puri, an Indian actor, plays the part of George Khan in *East Is East*. In this article he describes the character of George.

'As his world falls apart around him, George's only refuge is in the centuries-old traditions into which he was born. He is not a man who can break with his own experience and accept ideas and concepts that are alien to his upbringing.' [...]

The mixture of drama and comedy intrinsic to *East Is East* strongly attracted Om: 'There are a lot of dramatic moments as well as funny ones. This is reflected in George – he is both monstrously authoritarian and gently comic. It seems to me that he is a product of generation upon generation of tradition and he is neither strong enough nor educated enough to break out of this mindset.'

Om understood what makes George react to his wife and children in the way he does: 'Imagine the humiliation he feels in front of his community when Nazir runs out of his wedding in front of everyone and even worse, they find out he's in a gay relationship with a Frenchman! He can't accept it and it eats away at him. Then when all the other children start to disobey him, he blows up. He can't beat any of them in an argument because they're better at it than him, he doesn't have the mental capacity so he uses his fists.'

Om believes that George is something of an innocent: 'Like when he buys the barber's chair, he's really proud of it, so proud that he offers it to Mr Shah to sit on. He also has some lovely moments with Ella when he is like a flirtatious teenager – it's at those times that you can see why Ella is attracted to him.'

From: www.eastiseast.co.uk

1 *refuge* shelter or protection from danger, trouble, etc.

3 *alien* (adj) strange, different

5 *intrinsic to sth.* belonging to sth.

10 *mindset* set of fixed ideas and attitudes

15 *eat away at sb.* make sb. very anxious and upset

1 COMPREHENSION State which aspects of Om Puri's description of George apply to the scenes you have already analysed.

2 SPEAKING Get together with a partner and discuss this view of George's character. Support your opinion with reference to other events from the film.

5.3 GEORGE'S IDEA OF FATHERHOOD

VIEWING Watch the sequence 01:11:17–01:13:41.

1 COMPREHENSION Summarize George's point of view in three sentences.

2 George claims to have the right to make decisions for his children.
   a From this scene and the rest of the movie, list examples of decisions that George wants to make for his children.
   b Tick the ones that your parents might like to make for you.
   c Discuss your results.

3 SPEAKING Get together in groups of four and choose one of the following situations for a role-play:
   - George is furious and complains about Tariq to Ella.
   - Tariq comes back and wants to make his point once again.
   a Divide the group in two. Each half collects arguments for one of the characters involved.
   b Get together in pairs who have collected arguments for different persons. Act out your argument.

TIP

During the role-play, use discussion tickets:
Choose one useful phrase from each of the boxes below and write them on a card:

I believe … The way I see it, … It's a fact that … If you ask me … Well, I'd say …
I agree. You're quite right. Certainly. Definitely.
I'm not so sure, really. That doesn't convince me at all. It's not as simple as that.

Keep the cards in your hand during the role-play. Put down a card after you have used the phrase. Make sure to use all the phrases on your cards.

6 ELLA KHAN

6.1 VIEWING FOUR SEQUENCES

LISTENING Watch the following sequences, then tick the sentence that summarizes each sequence best.

1 0:19:14 – 0:19:59

	a George complains about Ella being lazy.
X	b Ella reminds George of how much she contributes to his quality of life.
	c Ella wants George to bring his first wife to help in the chip shop.

↳ economic

2 0:24:13 – 0:25:25

	a Ella explains to Annie why the circumcision was necessary.
X	b Ella has self-doubts about being a good mother.
	c Annie tries to console Ella and Sajid after the circumcision.

3 0:27:11 – 0:28:04

X	a Ella thinks George spent too much money on a useless present.
	b Ella is happy about the present George bought.
	c Ella cannot relax in the presence of George.

4 1:26:31 – 1:27:17

X	a Ella warns her children to respect their father.
	b Ella is fed up with her kids' troubles.
? X	c Ella feels that she can ~~neither~~ meet neither George's needs nor their children's.

6.2 VIEWING – A THINK–PAIR–SHARE ACTIVITY

1 **Think:** What does each of the sequences (cf. p. 27) tell you about Ella? Make notes.

2 **Pair:** Compare results with a partner, then write down which roles Ella seems to play and what problems she might have.

3 **Share** your ideas in class.

6.3 LINDA BASSETT ON ELLA KHAN

Linda Bassett, who plays Ella's part in the film, gives her view on Ella:

Ella has a strong belief in freedom, fairness, family … and Salford.

Ella is ferociously protective of her kids. She's learnt that society is hostile to them and also that their father is not prepared to allow them the freedom she herself feels they should have. So she spends a lot of her life fighting for them or keeping things from George to protect them from his anger.

I think Ella is like someone who lives under an oppressive regime – she has had to develop cunning, she is sometimes passive, sometimes aggressive and will do anything to make allies. One thing she has above George is that she sees her situation with clarity. He believes that moving to Bradford would solve their problems but Ella knows that the Pakistani community there, especially the women, will never accept her. This is why she has insisted on staying in Salford. Friendships with women are vital to her, with the affection and support they bring, and without Annie, Ella would perish.

From: www.eastiseast.co.uk

7 *cunning* (n) ability to trick or deceive others

9 *Bradford* city in Yorkshire with a large Pakistani population

13 *perish* die

1 COMPREHENSION List the aspects of the description of Ella that apply to the scenes you have already analysed.

2 WRITING Write an email to Linda Bassett in which you comment on her view of Ella.

7 RELIGION AND CULTURE

7.1 WORKING WITH WORDS

In the first segment of *East Is East* you saw two religious ceremonies – a Catholic procession and a Muslim wedding.

1 Make sure you understand all the words in the box below. Use a monolingual dictionary if necessary.

Useful vocabulary:

altar • arranged marriage • cathedral • ceremony • chant • choir • church • clergyman • cross • crucifix • dome • festivity • festival • holiday • hymn • minaret • mosque • mullah • parade • prayer • priest • procession • saint • sari • service • shalwar kameez • skullcap • spire • statue • turban • veil • vicar • wedding

2 Decide whether the words and phrases belong to a Christian or a Muslim context or to both. Write them in the relevant columns in the table below.

Christian	Muslim	both

7.2 TWO CEREMONIES

VIEWING Watch the beginning of the movie (0:00:00 – 0:09:23).

1 Choose either the procession or the wedding, then write a paragraph describing the event. Use as much of the new vocabulary from p. 29 as you can.

2 ANALYSIS Analyse how colour, sound and camera techniques (cf. Selected Terms for Film Analysis, p. 47) work together to create
   a a relaxed and cheerful atmosphere during the procession
   b a tense and uneasy atmosphere before and during the wedding ceremony.

First make notes in the table below.

Scene	Colour	Sound	Camera
Process.	muted ~: brown, grey + red brick	non-diegetic "The Banner Man" → relaxed playful	close-ups for people's feelings → different → lively atmosphere
Wedding	bright colours (golden, blue) cheerful ↔	Asian theme → reinforces dramatic events	
Prep.	dramatic development / sad	stops suddenly "expectant silence"	many close-ups → fear/panic/shock

8 IMMIGRANT CULTURE

8.1 GEORGE'S ARRIVAL IN BRITAIN

VIEWING Watch sequence 00:27:44-00:31:48. in the car!

1 LISTENING Listen carefully and fill in the gaps. Some require a word, others a longer phrase.

George: I come to ___this country___ in 1937.

I here maybe ___One year___ and I make a bloody ___film___.

Meenah: Were you ___the star___, Dad? [...]

George: No bloody ___star___, stupid. I was shouting in

a bloody ___crowd___: 'I ___kill___ bloody English.'

When I ___come this country___, I have ___no luggage___.

Today what I got?

Meenah: You've got ___a chip shop___, Dad.

George: Yes, ___own bloody brothers___.

2 WRITING Rewrite the dialogue as a grammatically correct dialogue between an educated English-speaking father and his daughter.

____

____

____

____

____

____

____

____

____

8.2 IMPRESSIONS OF THE PAKISTANI COMMUNITY

VIEWING Watch sequence 00:27:44 – 00:31:48 again.

1 ANALYSIS Analyse how British and immigrant culture are contrasted and explain the function of the town sign.

2 ANALYSIS Examine the impressions of 'Bradistan' conveyed in the sequence. Choose vocabulary from the box below. Make sure to use suitable verbs and/or prepositions with the nouns to form idiomatic phrases, e.g. 'doing business in the market' etc.

Useful vocabulary:

aromatic • Asian • bright • busy • business • colourful • dressed • exotic • foreign • gaudy • happy • hectic • imported • lively • scented • spicy • strange • clothing • customers • food • market • produce • shop • smell(s) • spices • stall • vegetables

3 ANALYSIS Examine the atmosphere conveyed in the sequence and analyse how it is created (cf. Selected Terms for Film Analysis, p. 47).

4 ANALYSIS Describe the still below (cf. How to Analyse Film Stills, p. 56) and examine in what way the film language underlines its message.

00:32:09

9 A QUESTION OF PERSPECTIVE – ANALYSING FILM LANGUAGE

1 ANALYSIS The filmmaker presents his storyline from many different perspectives.

a **Think:** Think of one sequence with a striking camera perspective that you remember well. Analyse the camera range, camera perspective, and camera angle and make notes on your results.

b **Pair:** Describe your sequence and the cinematic devices you have considered to a partner. Together describe the effects these cinematic devices might have on the audience.

c **Share:** In class, present and discuss your results.

2 ANALYSIS Analyse the significance of the camera perspective in the following shots.

A 00:14:48

Sajid's eye-level / close-ups
- put in Sajid's shoes

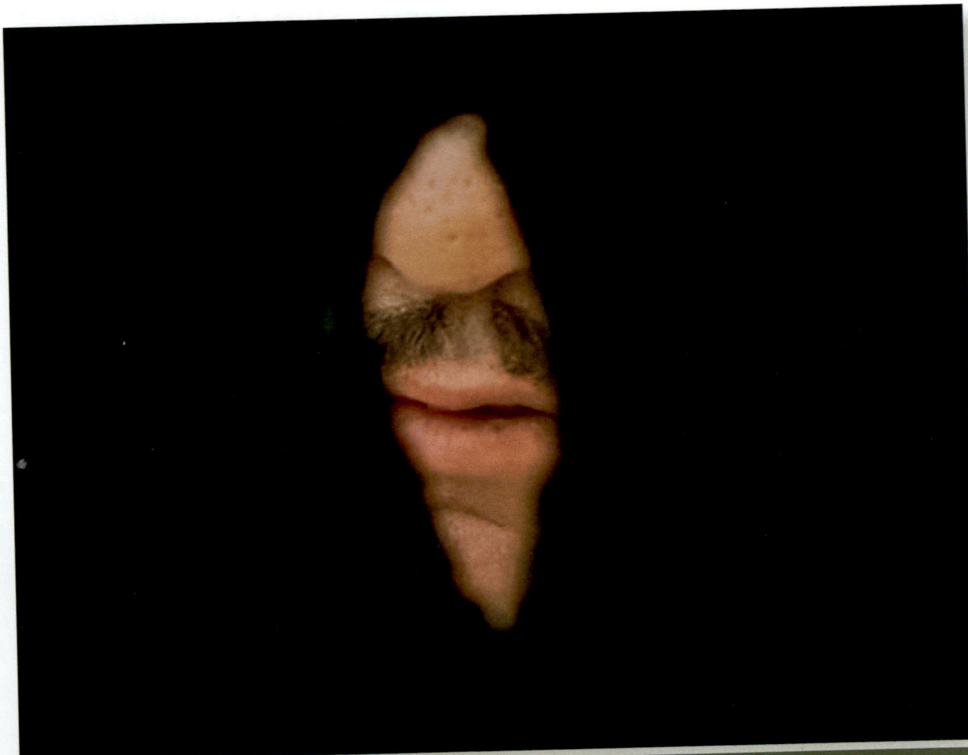

B 00:18:54

extreme close-up

3 ANALYSIS Sajid, the youngest son, usually wears a parka. At the end of the movie, the hood is ripped off accidentally and Sajid does not put it back on. Discuss the relevance of the parka for Sajid and the implications of his behaviour at the end of the movie.

Useful vocabulary:

stand for sth. • represent sth. • associate sth. with sth. • hint at sth. • allude to sth. • be a symbol of sth.

4 WRITING Imagine Sajid later explains to his friend Earnest why he does not wear the parka any longer. With a partner, write the dialogue between the two boys. You may want to act it out in class.

- hides from conflicts   parka = shield (protects him from … + his identity)

- ripped-off hood - exposure to reality
- does not want the hood back on
⇒ ability has grown to face the world outside
emancipation → growing up

10 THE ENDING – TALKING ABOUT EMOTIONS

VIEWING Watch sequence 1:13:48 – 1:30:00.

1 SPEAKING In pairs discuss how you reacted to
- the conversation with the Shahs in the Khans' sitting-room
- Saleem's sudden interruption with his 'work of art'
- the subsequent sequences of open clashes, suffering and reconciliation
- the final street sequences, again involving the 'work of art'.

Useful vocabulary:

positive	neutral	negative
amused	disinterested	annoyed
contented	unconcerned	depressed
excited		disappointed
fascinated		disgusted
pleased		embarrassed
relieved		frustrated
satisfied		full of pity
thrilled		worried
surprised		irritated
sympathetic (towards)		uneasy

2 Match the verbs and nouns from the table below to make meaningful collocations. Write the numbers to the corresponding letters in the right column. Use your monolingual dictionary if necessary. Some nouns may go with more than one verb.

Verb		Noun		Possible collocations	
A	arouse	1	interest	A	
B	ease	2	tension	B	
C	provoke	3	criticism	C	
D	express	4	comic relief	D	
E	evoke	5	amusement	E	
F	provide	6	irony	F	
G	employ	7	sympathy for	G	
H	build up	8	pity for	H	
I	utter	9	curiosity	I	
		10	entertainment		
		11	a reaction		
		12	anger		
		13	humour		

3 WRITING Write an analysis of the final sequence (ca. 200 words) with particular emphasis on the emotions presented in it and their effect on the viewer. Make sure to use at least five collocations from task 2.

PART VI POST-VIEWING ACTIVITIES

1 A PROBLEM OF IDENTITY

1 Identities
   a How would you define identity? Make a cluster of your ideas. Check a monolingual dictionary and write a clear definition of the term.

2 In a review (cf. p. 41) the writer says about George that he 'feels as though he's betraying his roots'. What might these roots be?

3 Choose one of the children as 'your' character and from their point of view write either a poem titled 'Who am I?' or an acrostic (see below) using either your character's name or the word *identity*.

Example: An acrostic for George

		a	g	G	r	e	s	s	i	v	e				
		u	n	E	e	d	u	c	a	t	e	d			
		r	o	O	t	s	-	o	r	i	e	n	t	e	d
		t	o	R	m	e	n	t	e	d					
i	m	m	i	G	r	a	n	t							
v	i	o	l	E	n	t									

2 A QUICK CHAT WITH AYUB KHAN-DIN *Mark Olden*

The following questions and answers are taken from an interview with Ayub Khan-Din, the writer of the screenplay of *East Is East*.

1 Match the questions with the answers by filling the correct letter in the right column of the table.

Question	Answer
How did you get into writing?	F
What was your involvement with the film?	C
Just how autobiographical is *East Is East*?	A
Among the film's running themes are the India-Pakistan war and Enoch Powell. Are they particularly vivid memories for you?	B
Do you have any expectations of how the film will be received in the more traditional parts of the Asian community?	E
Do you think the pressures on young Asians living between the pull of different cultures are less severe than when you were growing up?	D

A The parents are drawn directly from my own family. The youngest boy, Sajid, is me as a child. All the arguments in the film, all the theories behind the father's way of thinking, are my own arguments and theories, which I developed from writing the first draft of the stageplay to the last draft of the screenplay. The different issues, the different aspects of different relationships – they're all very similar to my own background.

B When all these events started happening, I was Sajid. I was living in a parka. Enoch Powell was always being thrown in my face as a child, and the whole Bangladesh war of independence had a big effect on our household because what happened in the house always revolved around the TV news. In a way, it was almost as if the disintegration of Pakistan was happening in our house at the same time. It affected everything that was going on.

C I was involved right from day one, and reserved the right to say yes or no.

D To a certain extent it's gone full circle. In Bradford it's gone from being traditional to being modern, and back to being traditional again. Because Pakistanis have not seen themselves accepted in this country and have faced racism, along with unemployment and riots, the younger generation has rebelled against the older one and said that they have become too modern and too accepting. You have to find a balance. When you decide to move to a country, you have to understand that your children are going to

9 *Bangladesh* war revolution in East Pakistan that resulted in the independence of the People's Republic of Bangladesh (March – December 1971)

11 *disintegration of Pakistan* process of Pakistan splitting up into Pakistan and Bangladesh in 1971

14 *go full circle* (of a situation) develop in a certain direction and then back to how it started

17 *riot* violent behaviour in public of a group of people, often as a protest be influenced by the culture of that country. I think most of the young Asians have found a happy balance, taking the best and leaving the rest of each culture. There will always be traditional families and there will always be the kind of problems my brothers and sisters faced. It'll never go away.

E I've made a point in the film of not making it offensive or irreligious at all, so there's nothing they can point to. It's like walking on egg shells. I'm sure people will have some criticism about how I portray my father. But at the end of the day, I'm portraying my father, he's not a Pakistani everyman. To a certain extent, this is a man who abandoned his culture and married an English woman, and then decided that his children should marry Pakistanis. So you know, there was huge hypocrisy there. I made a point of not going to any Q&A sessions after the play because I didn't want to have to start justifying what I'd written. It was a personal story. I wasn't writing about any specific community, I was writing about my father.

F When I left school mid 70s, I was thick as two short planks. I managed to scrape three CSEs: Biology, Religious Knowledge and Art. I hated school and I was a bit thick. So I got me a job as a hairdresser and I was the worst hairdresser in Manchester. I never got further than sweeping the floor and washing people's hair. One day, in the hairdresser's, I picked up David Niven's book, *The Moon's a Balloon*, and read that he went from being in the army to being an actor. So I thought if someone can go from one diverse job to another, why can't I? So I just rang the local college, Salford Tech, and asked if they did a drama course. They asked what qualifications I had and just laughed. But I got in and started writing *East Is East* there.

From: www.kamera.co.uk

31 *hypocrisy* behaviour in which sb. pretends to have moral standards or opinions that they do not really have

32 *Q&A* question and answer

35 *(as) thick as two short planks* (infml) very stupid

36 *scrape sth.* get sth. with difficulty

36 *CSE* (formerly in GB) exams which a pupil took when he or she was 16

39 *David Niven* (1910–1983) English Hollywood actor

2 COMPREHENSION State how autobiographical the film is.

personal story (33)
similar to his own background (5)
felt like Sajid (8)

3 COMPREHENSION Outline how representative the film is of Pakistani culture in Britain, according to Khan-Din. Make sure to discuss Khan-Din's statement 'I wasn't writing about any specific community, I was writing about my father' (ll. 33 f.).

partially representative of Pakis living in B. in 1970s

4 SPEAKING Khan-Din says 'most of the young Asians have found a happy balance, taking the best and leaving the rest of each culture' (ll. 22 f.) Prepare an interview with a friend or a family member with a multi-ethnic background to find out how their identity is shaped by their respective cultures.

a Develop a questionnaire with at least three questions, and then conduct the interview.

b Note down your interviewee's responses and report these to the class. Make sure to use indirect speech.

3 IMMIGRATION – IT'S UP FOR A DEBATE

SPEAKING Prepare and conduct a discussion about immigration.

1 Divide the class into two groups. One group collects arguments for the benefits of immigration, the other group deals with its risks. Use information from the film and the texts you have read, but add your own ideas as well.

2 Decide on the form of the discussion, e. g. debate, fish bowl, or American debate (cf. p. 39). If necessary, prepare a statement/motion to start with. Choose students to play the role of moderator, chairperson and/or timekeeper if necessary.

3 Hold the discussion. Make sure to use appropriate vocabulary for a discussion.

Useful vocabulary:

Giving an opinion/ Emphasizing	Agreeing/Defending one's point	Disagreeing/Arguing against sth.
In my opinion ... To my mind ... I am (strongly) convinced that ... I am of the opinion that ... I strongly believe that ... I would like to emphasize that ... There is strong evidence that ...	I (totally) agree. Exactly. Absolutely. That is definitely true (but ...) You are certainly right (but ...) You have a point there (but ...) I see your point (but ...)	I (completely) disagree (with you on ...) I think you are wrong. I am sorry but I don't agree at all. I strongly criticize ... I don't think/believe that ... I think you are mistaken when ... I would question that argument.

INFOBOX | An American Debate

- Students work in two groups. One group collects arguments *for*, the other group arguments *against* a topic. Each group should try to anticipate the other group's arguments and ways to refute them.
- In the debate, the groups sit in two lines facing each other.
- First a speaker from group A presents their arguments, then a speaker from group B etc. (see diagram on the right).
- Each speaker may only speak for a limited time (usually about 60 seconds).
- A moderator strictly observes the debate.
- After both groups have finished, there should be time for reflection.

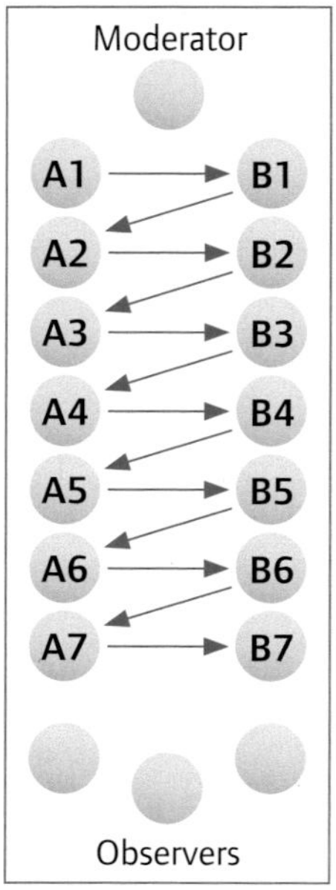

Modifications: In the first round, the speakers take turns to present one argument after the other without referring to the other group's arguments. After all the arguments have been presented, the students discuss within their own group how to refute the other group's arguments.
In the second round speakers from group A and B take turns, this time referring to the other's arguments and presenting counterarguments before adding another argument.

Round 1:

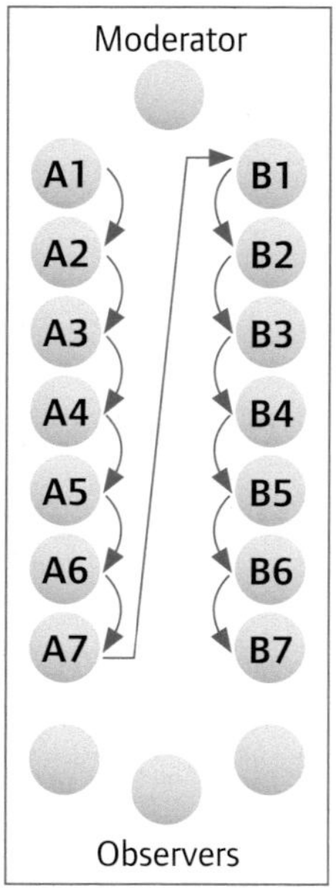

Round 2:

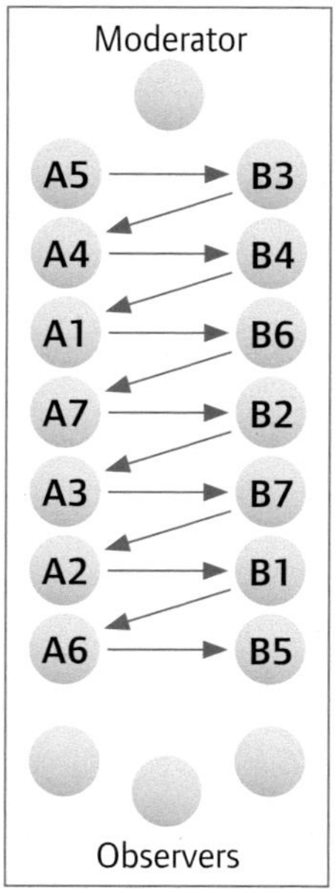

ABI Revision!

4 A REVIEW

1 In the text below, certain passages have been left … the letters A–E. Read the text, then identify the c… gaps in the table below. Write the correct letter in … ending you won't need.

1	understanding how much Saleem (Chris Biss… at art school, turning a blind eye to Tariq's (J… rebellious dalliances at the local disco.	
2	but proves reluctant to allow his progeny the… make their own mistakes.	
3	and then it becomes serious; sometimes that'… events pan out.	
4	yet after 25 years it still feels as though he's betraying his roots.	
5	and that is what makes the characters so convincing.	
6	a reaction against his nature but realistic in context.	

East Is East DAMIAN CANNON

George Khan (Om Puri) is one of these ghosts; long domiciled in England he remains unable to reconcile his internal conflicts. By marrying northern lass Ella (Linda Bassett) he should have been welcomed into society, **A** That's why George tries to rule his large family with an iron fist, brooking no argument or dissension. He needs to be accepted by the Salford Pakistani population, so George aims to make amends through his offspring. The crux of is that they don't want to be good Pakistanis, they just want to be themselves. However, when eldest son Nazir (Ian Aspinall) makes this plain by fleeing at the altar, George's mind is set; the Khan tribe will endure no more disgrace.

What brings it all together for is superior acting by every single cast member. From the start they move as one body, moderating emotional pitch in synchronisation, just like a real family. George is no monster, merely a stubborn father reacting to circumstance by retreating into authoritarian tradition. Ella views the tribe from another perspective, **B** She allows Meenah (Archie Panjabi) to be a tomboy, lets quiet Abdul (Raji James) get on with life, loves devout Maneer (Emil Marwa) even as he attempts to obey George through religion. Moreover, Ella adores identity-confused Sajid (Jordan Routledge) as he hides in his sweaty parka.

This is a story firmly rooted in Salford's terraced streets, kids playing in the road, outdoor lavatories and George's chippie being where you eat once

1 *'these ghosts'* reference to the first paragraph of the review, in which Cannon speaks of people who do not belong anywhere

1 *domiciled* (fml) living

2 *lass* (Northern English dialect) young woman

4 *brook no …* not accept sth.

5 *dissension* disagreement

6 *make amends* etwas wiedergutmachen

6 *offspring* children

12 *pitch* strength of sth., e.g. a feeling

14 *tribe* Volksstamm

15 *tomboy* girl who behaves like a boy

16 *devout* strongly religious

a week. An old-fashioned community that lags behind modern mores, it becomes lovingly rendered by . This setting, just down the road from Bradford, centre of Indian culture, is perfect for Ayub Khan-Din's closely observed study. It allows him, through director Damien O'Donnell, to pick up on the details of their cramped life; buckets for night-time urination, kids three to a bed, biscuits for breakfast. There's great humour here, in the sibling insults and snatched back-alley kisses. At times the movie is so funny it hurts, leaving you wracked in wonderful agony, (C).

For claims to be neither comedy nor tragedy, but a reflection of the gulf that separates first and second generations. George dreams that his adopted home offers opportunities unavailable elsewhere, (D). George thinks that he wants respect, when he's really asking for submission before his vision of a true Pakistani. The kids can only attempt to draw the best from multiple cultures, attaining a personal balance while avoiding their father's provoked wrath. Against a background of Enoch Powell and subtle prejudice (even against other subcontinent immigrants) they're treading a delicate line.

Fundamentally is a film about tolerance for views that rub against your own. It shows how George, unable to channel frustration constructively, boils over into violence; (E). It also shows how Ella is torn between her love for George and her desire to protect and encourage their children, another difficult position. The charm of is its sympathy to the characters and their divisions, to the reality that great emotional resolutions do not in practice occur. Superb ensemble acting by the small-name cast ensures that you're gripped from beginning to end by their full, warm performances. Even better, Khan-Din both translates his stage play faithfully and transforms it to make use of cinema's visual possibilities. Altogether a great night out.

21 *mores* (pl) (fml) typical customs and behaviour of a particular group

28 *wracked with sth.* (usu. racked) suffering a lot

32 *submission* act of accepting that you must obey sb./sth.

35 *wrath* extreme anger

36 *tread a delicate line* be in a difficult situation where you could easily make mistakes

43 *small-name cast* not very well-known actors

From: www.film.u-net.com

2 WRITING Write a letter to the editor in which you comment on the critic's opinion of the movie (about 200 words).

5 TWO REVIEWS – MEDIATION

You are planning to go to the cinema with an English-speaking friend at the weekend. You have found out that *West is West* is on, the sequel to *East Is East*. Since you liked *East Is East* very much, you now consider watching *West is West*. In order to inform yourself and provide your friend with some information about the film, you read two film reviews.

MEDIATION Write your friend an email. It should contain
- relevant facts about the film
- a summary of the plot
- the critics' opinions of the film
- a clear suggestion either to watch the film or not
- about 250 words.

Multikulti-Komödie "West is West": Klischee ist Klischee

DANIEL SANDER

Der Zauber ist verflogen: 1999 war die Komödie „East Is East" über den chaotischen Alltag einer britisch-pakistanischen Familie in England ein Überraschungshit. Nun schickt die Fortsetzung „West is West" die Helden von damals in die pakistanische Heimat. Keine gute Idee.

Der Erfolg [von „East Is East"] war so groß, dass es erstaunlich ist, dass die Fortsetzung mehr als zehn Jahre auf sich warten ließ. Doch in der Filmwelt von „West is West" sind nur vier Jahre vergangen: Familienoberhaupt Zahir „George" Khan (Om Puri) ist immer noch einigermaßen glücklich mit Ella (Linda Bassett) verheiratet und betreibt in Salford einen Fish-and-Chips-Laden. Bei den meisten seiner sieben Kinder hat er die Hoffnung aufgegeben, dass aus ihnen noch brave Muslime mit Sinn für Tradition und Moral werden, aber noch nicht bei seinem Jüngsten, dem 15-jährigen Sajid (Aqib Khan). Der zeigt sich gerade besonders aufmüpfig und kompensiert das ständige Mobbing seiner Mitschüler und Lehrer mit ein bisschen Ladendiebstahl.

Und weil George immer noch einen Hang dazu hat, völlig undurchdachte Ideen überstürzt in die Tat umzusetzen, verschleppt er seinen Sohn nach Pakistan, um ihm etwas über sein kulturelles Erbe beizubringen. Für Unterschlupf ist gesorgt, denn schließlich hat George ja noch eine erste Ehefrau samt Tochter vor Ort. Dass die nicht gerade vor Begeisterung umfallen, als er vor der Tür steht, ist für ihn ganz und gar unbegreiflich.

Eigentlich gute Voraussetzungen dafür, ein bisschen von der Magie des ersten Teils in die Fortsetzung hinüber zu retten, denn Gelegenheiten für überdrehten Slapstick sollten bei so viel Kulturkampf so reichlich vorhanden sein wie tiefschürfende Erkenntnisse über Moral. Das Problem ist nur, dass „West is West" sich so furchtbar anstrengt, für beides zu sorgen. Obwohl die Kernbesetzung dieselbe blieb (abgesehen vom 15-jährigen Sajid), und das

Drehbuch wieder vom britisch-pakistanischen Schauspieler und Autor Ayub Khan-Din stammt, ist von der süffisanten Leichtigkeit aus „East Is East" nicht mehr viel zu spüren.

Der neue Regisseur Andy DeEmmony hat keinen Sinn für den zurückgenommenen Tonfall seines Vorgängers Damian O'Donnell und inszeniert das Ganze als brachiale Mischung aus Billig-Sitcom und TV-Movie. Es ist alles zu viel, und nichts wirkt echt: Sajid ist ein so penetrant aufgeweckter und pseudo-rebellischer Teenager, wie es sie nur in Drehbüchern gibt, immer einen gewollt respektlosen Spruch auf den Lippen. Sein Vater ist vom zwiespältigen Charakter zum kompletten Monster geworden, dessen Egomanie und unsagbare Dummheit für Spaß sorgen sollen, aber nur noch verachtenswert sind.

Manchmal wirkt es so, als wollte der Regisseur die große Liste der Kino-Klischees abarbeiten: Erst ein unbeteiligter, weiser alter Mann schafft es, Sajids Herz für die Heimat zu öffnen; ohne die Sprache der jeweils anderen zu verstehen, kommt es zwischen Georges zwei Ehefrauen zur betont herzerweichenden Aussprache; ein Sturm bringt im Finale alle in Gefahr und Vater und Sohn wieder näher zueinander; jeder hat am Ende eine wichtige Lektion gelernt.

Es ist ein bisschen traurig. „West is West" will auch ein Film sein, den jeder mag, wie das Original, und er versucht es mit allen Mitteln. Dabei weiß doch jeder, dass man so nur allen auf die Nerven geht.

From: www.spiegel.de

West is West Anke Sternborg

Nach zwölf Jahren findet der britische Publikumshit *East Is East* eine Fortsetzung, die in der Originalheimat der Familie spielt, wohin George „Genghis" Khan (wieder von Om Puri verkörpert) Sohn Sajid bringt. 1999 ging es in *East Is East* um die Probleme, die die pubertierenden britischen Jungs mit ihrem pakistanischen Vater und seinem rigiden Traditionsbewusstsein in der nordenglischen Kleinstadt Salford hatten. Aus der Reibung zwischen allgemeingültigen Immigrantenproblemen und individuellem Zeit- und Ortskolorit, zwischen englischer Arbeiterklasse und indisch-pakistanischer Kultur schlug der Film ebenso komische wie herzzerreißende Funken. Die Geschichte speiste sich aus den intimen Lebenserfahrungen des pakistanischen Engländers Ayub Khan-Din und wurde zum weltweiten Hit. Rund 12 Jahre später folgt nun ein Sequel, das die Gefahren, zum lauen Abklatsch der Originalstory zu werden, mit einem simplen Trick umschifft.

Der jüngste Sohn der Familie Khan macht Schwierigkeiten, allerdings nur weil er als „schmutziger Paki" in der Schule gemobbt wird. Kurzerhand beschließt der Vater (großartig bärbeißig: Om Puri), ihn mit seinen fremden Wurzeln im indischen Punjab vertraut zu machen, und wie es sich für jeden anständigen Pubertierenden gehört, will Sajid davon gar nichts wissen. Es dauert eine Weile, ehe er vor Ort einer äußerst wirksamen Éducation sentimentale erliegt und die harte Schale des muffigen Pubertisten durch die weisen Ratschläge eines alten Philosophen und die Aufmunterungen eines gleichaltrigen Jungen erweicht wird. Eine furiose Schnittfolge, in der die beiden Jungs auf den Dächern der kleinen Häuser hinter den unten über die Straßen flirrenden Frauen hinterherjagen, vermittelt die flirrende Energie des indischen Alltags.

Aus der britischen Perspektive von *East Is East* war die pakistanische Familie, die der Patriarch verlassen hatte, um alsbald in England eine neue zu gründen, ein vages Feindbild, das schwarze Loch, in dem ein großer Teil des sauer in der Frittenbude verdienten Geldes verschwand. Nun wechselt der Film den Blickwinkel, tut voller Herz und Humor einen erhellenden Blick hinter den Vorhang der Vorurteile und Vorwürfe. Aber auch George „Genghis" Khan wird in den Sog seines alten Lebens gezogen, während er ein Haus zu bauen beginnt, vergisst er schnell seine britische Frau, die eines Tages überraschend mit ihrer Freundin aus dem Taxi steigt, um nach dem Rechten zu sehen. Was alsbald als Zickenkrieg unter den beiden Khan-Frauen beginnt, entwickelt sich schleichend zu einer sachten Annäherung. Während beide Frauen bisher immer gramvoll der Meinung waren, die jeweils andere habe das bessere, einfachere Los gezogen, stellt sich nun schnell raus, dass das Gras in Wirklichkeit nirgends grüner ist. So bringt die spontane Reise Bewegung in alle verhärteten Situationen, auf unterschiedliche Weise erleben der Vater und seine mehr oder weniger erwachsenen Söhne ebenso wie seine geplagten Frauen eine durchaus berührende Bewusstwerdung, während Indien für einen guten Schuss Farbe, Energie und Lebensfreude sorgt, die dem Film über Kamera, Kostüme und Musik ganz selbstverständlich injiziert werden. Wenn die britischen Ladies in ihren knalligen Seventies-Polyester-Outfits aus dem Taxi steigen, bahnt sich hinter dem Clash der Kulturen schon farblich die Völkerverständigung an.

From: www.epd-film.de

PART VII EXAM TASKS

Tasks similar to the following might occur in written exams. You may choose to complete one or more tasks from each section to prepare for exams.

Comprehension

1 Summarize the film in about 250 words.

2 Describe George's and Ella's roles in the family.

3 Outline the children's problems.

Analysis

1 Examine George's behaviour towards Ella.

2 Explain Ella's dilemma.

3 Compare Ella's and George's attitudes towards the education of their children.

4 Analyse the relevance of the setting for the storyline.

5 Examine to what degrees the Khans have integrated into British society.

6 Choose three of the minor characters in the film (e.g. Annie, Stella, Ernest, Ernest's grandfather, etc.). Examine the function they have in the film.

7 Analyse the use of different camera perspectives and their effect on the viewer.

8 Compare the presentation of culture clash in the film to other texts with which you have dealt.

Comment / Composition / Creative Writing

1 Comment on George's attempts influence his children's future.

2 Assess to what extent the film is successful in depicting the problems of first- and second-generation immigrants.

3 After their visit to the Khan's house the Shahs discuss what has happened and how they feel about it. Write a dialogue between Mr and Mrs Shah.

4 Nazir and his father meet again a few months later. Write a dialogue in which Nazir explains his way of life and why he left the family.

5 Write a blog entry in which you discuss both the advantages and disadvantages of growing up in a multi-ethnic family.

PART VIII FILM STUDIES: EXTRAS

1 SELECTED TERMS FOR FILM ANALYSIS

Camera range/kinds of shot	The distance between camera and object
close shot	In a **close shot** a person's face, shoulders and part of his/her arm are shown.
close-up 	An entire human face from chin or lower neck to top of head fills the frame. Shows the finest nuances of expression.
extreme close-up 	Parts of the face (or object) fill the entire frame.
medium shot 	Characters and surroundings are shown at a moderate size, with characters seen from mid-body up. It is usually chosen to show one or two characters in action.
full shot 	Includes the entire body of a character and not much else. The **full shot** is used to emphasize action and the constellation of characters.
long shot 	Characters and surroundings are shown from a distance and in their entirety. It is usually used to introduce a new setting (see **establishing shot**) to show characters in relation to the action, to show movement over large distances, or to juxtapose different characters within one frame.

Camera perspective	
establishing shot	A **long shot** that establishes a setting, scene or mood; frequently used at the beginning of a scene.
over-the-shoulder shot	A shot taken with the camera placed behind a character who is only partially seen, looking over his/her shoulder. Usually used in dialogue scenes, showing the dialogue partner from the second character's point of view.
point-of-view shot	Also known as 'subjective camera'. A shot taken with the camera placed approximately where the character's eyes would be in order to depict a scene from the visual or emotional perspective of one of the characters.
shot/reverse shot **reverse-angle shot**  	A **shot/reverse shot** is an **over-the-shoulder shot** followed by a **reverse-angle shot**. A **reverse-angle shot** is a shot in which the angle is opposite to that in the preceding shot.
Camera angle	
eye-level shot/ **straight-on angle** 	A shot filmed at eye level.
high-angle shot 	A shot filmed from above the object; may be used to diminish the character's importance.
low-angle shot 	Filmed from below the object, a **low-angle shot** may be used to underline the importance or power of a character or object. Shown as a **point-of-view shot**, it indicates fear or respect on the part of the character viewing a particular scene.

Camera movement	
crane shot 	A shot filmed from a crane that can move the camera in any direction. It is almost always linked to another movement of the camera, such as a **pan** or **tilt**, in which case it becomes a compound movement.
hand-held camera	A filming technique in which the camera is held by the operator during a take.
pan/panning shot 	The camera moves horizontally from left to right or vice versa (**pan** right or **pan** left). A **panning shot** is often used to follow a character's movement or to indicate a **point-of-view shot** with the character looking around or searching for something.
tilt/tilt shot	The camera moves vertically upward or downward. A **tilt shot** is often used to indicate height or follow a character or object moving up or downwards, e.g. a leaf dropping.
tracking shot 	Camera movement in which the entire camera is moved either forward, backward, laterally, or in a circular or irregular pattern. The camera is placed on a movable device (a camera dolly) moving along pre-laid tracks or is moved freely along a level surface (hand-held camera or steady cam). In a **tracking shot**, the camera range may either remain constant, following along next to or behind a moving character or object, or it may be used to get closer to or further away from the target object in a manner similar to a **zoom** shot. Usually used to indicate steady movement through the setting, e.g. indicating a character running or two characters walking together.
zoom	The stationary camera appears to approach a character or object by **zooming in** or to move farther away by **zooming out**.
Editing terms	**The arrangement of shots in a structured sequence**
cross-cutting/ parallel action	Also known as parallel editing. An editing technique that alternates shots of two or more actions occurring in different places at the same time. Usually used to follow multiple plot lines, to compare or to juxtapose different actions or settings, or to show different reactions to a particular event.
cut	Transition from one shot to another. The most basic editing technique for connecting two shots within a scene and between scenes.
jump-cut	A (very) abrupt transition from one shot to another eleminating one strip of action and creating an effect of disorientation or rapid movement.

match cut	A technique in which two shots are linked by the same acting or by some form of visual parallelism. The two shots seem to continue uninterrupted, e.g. one door closing and then another door opening. **Match cuts** can be used to underline a connection between two separate elements. Often used to create a smooth flow between two scenes or, if using the same character in the action, to mark the passing of time.
dissolve	A transition between two shots created by gradually overlapping the last shot of a scene with the first shot of the next scene. This is done by superimposing a **fade-out** onto a **fade-in** of equal length. Often this transition is used to underline the connection between two scenes or to indicate a change of location or the passing of time.
fade-in **fade-out**	A transition between two shots. The last image of one scene gradually disappears from the screen (**fade-out**) to be replaced by a monochrome screen, and the first shot of the next scene gradually brightens from a blank screen to the whole image (**fade-in**). Often used to indicate a passing of time (e.g. from night to day), or to mark the beginning and end of a dream sequence (**flashback** or **flash-forward**).
flashback	A filmed sequence that goes back in narrative time to show events that took place earlier than the present-time of the film. Usually used to provide expository material and to underline the feelings and motives of characters.
flash-forward	A filmed sequence that moves forward in narrative time to show events that take place later than the present-time of the film. Usually used to underline the presence of an omniscient narrator, a **flash-forward** shows the consequences of a certain action that the characters are still unaware of. It gives the audience the impression of knowing more than the characters.
Additional film terms	
arc shot	Camera movement in which the entire camera moves around a subject or object in a circle.
backlighting	Filming a person or event against a background of light, e.g. the sun. It may produce an idealized, sometimes romantic effect.
camera operator	The person behind the camera(s); in major productions, the head of the camera team is usually called the director of photography.
cast	All actors who appear in a film.
clapboard (US)/ **clapperboard** (GB) 	A small board which gives information about a film: e.g. the director, the director of photography, the scene, take number, date and time. It is filmed at the beginning of each take. It helps to identify all takes and cuts down continuity errors.

credits	The list of people who were involved in the making of a film or television programme.
director	The person responsible for the artistic production of a film, involving all its creative elements, e.g. camerawork, editing, and the actors' interpretation of their roles.
editor	(verb: edit) The person responsible for putting the camera shots together and arranging them into a finished product.
fade	Transition between two shots. The last image gradually disappears from the screen (**fade-out**) to be replaced by a monochrome screen, and the first shot of the next screen gradually brightens from a blank screen to the whole image (**fade-in**).
footage	A length of film made for TV or cinema.
frame	A single image of the film.
insert (shot)	A detail shot which quickly gives visual information necessary to understand the meaning of a scene, e.g. a newspaper page or a physical detail.
lighting	The creation of controlled illumination upon a scene or object to be filmed and thus the ultimate tool of the cinematographer. Light sources may be natural or artificial or both. If natural, the light may be directed onto the scene by reflecting devices. If artificial, it is of course aimed at the specific target area designated by the director of photography and channelled through the use of such devices as cookies, flags, and doors. The light may also be diffused or it may be sharply focused. If, as might be said, cinematography is painting with light, lighting is the palette which the painter uses. Though methods for lighting a scene are highly varied, the one most commonly used in conventional practice is known as the 'Three-Point Lighting System'.
high-key lighting **low-key lighting**	The intensity and sharpness of light and corresponding shadow (or lack of this) which illuminates a scene is described as being either **high** or **low key**. This is true irrespective of whether the film is monochromatic or in colour. Lighting that creates comparatively little contrast between the light and dark areas of the shot is **high-key**, lighting that creates strong contrast between the light and dark areas of the shot is **low-key lighting**.
location	See: set.
mise-en-scène	Literally translated from French, the phrase means 'put upon the stage'; otherwise known simply as 'staging'. In film-making the term has come to mean the totality of how the director designs and sets in motion a given scene. All films use essentially the same techniques and processes. However, each individual film employs all of the variable elements of production provided by the technology available in its own distinct way. The elements generally used to define and analyse **mise-en-scène** are: setting, actor placement, actor movement, actor interpretation (ideally, but not always a collaboration between director and actor), camera movement, costumes and make-up.
motion picture/movie	US and Canadian terms for film.

producer	The person responsible for the overall organization, especially the financing and marketing, of a film or television production.
scene	A shot or series of shots that deal with a single action (see also **sequence**).
score	Film music.
screenplay	The script of a film or television show, usually including dialogue as well as rough descriptions of the setting, camera distance, camera movements, etc.
sequence	A part of a film dealing with one or more scenes that form a single continuous episode.
set	The site or location where a film is being shot.
shot	A single piece of film, however long or short, taken by a single camera without cuts.
soundtrack	The audio equivalent of the picture or image track, the **soundtrack** contains all the audio information which accompanies the film: dialogue, music, sound effects, etc.
still	A single photograph or shot from a film.
storyboard	A **storyboard** is a useful tool in the creation of any media production. It is a series of sketches or still photographs that show how the different shots might look when filmed. It almost looks like a comic book of the film.
take	A single attempt to film a shot. Though sometimes confused with **shot**, there can in fact be an unlimited number of takes of the same shot until either the director is satisfied or the producer calls a halt.
top shot	Extreme **high-angle shot** where the camera looks straight down.
voice-over	An off-screen voice that gives the audience necessary background information. It is often used in documentaries. In a narrative film, this technique often implies a first-person or omniscient narrator's point of view.
wipe	Transitional device in which shot B seemingly moves in either screen direction across shot A, thus effectively wiping off shot A and replacing it.

2 WORKING WITH A FILM VIEWING LOG

You are probably used to keeping a reading log when studying a novel. When studying a film, it is even more important to take notes during the viewing process for future reference, as it is more difficult to go back to different parts of the film.

Before viewing
Find out all you can about the film you are going to see:

What genre does it belong to (e.g. feature film, documentary, video clip, newscast, commercial)? What country does it come from? When was it made? Are you going to see it in the original language (with or without subtitles), or is it a dubbed version? Was it made for television or for the cinema?

While viewing
Pay close attention to how visual and audio elements influence your reaction to the film:

- **Characters:** How does the film show you who the main characters are? What information do you get about them? What is their relationship to each other? What impression do they make on you, and why? Watch for facial expressions and body language that may convey important signals.
- **Setting:** How does the film let you know where the plot is set? What impression do you get of the setting? How do colour, music, lighting, background noise contribute to this impression?
- **Plot:** Is the plot introduced gradually (e.g. while the titles are being shown) or does the story begin in the middle and make the viewer draw conclusions based on indirect clues? Does it use flashbacks (or flash-forwards), or is the story told chronologically? Does the point of view of one character dominate, or does the film jump from one character to another? Is there one main plot, or does the film tell a series of loosely connected episodes? Are special effects used, and if so, to what effect?
- **Information:** Particularly in a documentary film, consider how the information presented to the viewer. Does the director use music to appeal to the emotions and convince his audience? Is slow motion used? If so, when and why?

Using a viewing log can help you to keep track of what you notice while watching a film or video sequence.

Your viewing log might look like the one below, but feel free to choose different categories to fit your own purposes:

What? (sequence/ scene)	When/Where?	Who?	Filmic devices	Comments/ Questions

After viewing

Go over your viewing log again and add information or comments. Think about your overall response to the film:

What emotions does the film arouse, and through what means? Do you identify with one or more of the characters, and if so, why? Does the film try to make you take sides, or does it encourage you to draw your own conclusions? Discuss these questions with others who have seen the film and analyse the reasons for your reactions. If possible, re-examine sequences/ scenes that provoked conflicting views and discuss why you respond to them in different ways.

3 HOW TO WRITE A FILM REVIEW

A film review is a written text that provides information about a film. It is intended either to recommend the film in question or to discourage people from seeing it. It can also help people to form their own opinion of the film.

- Start by considering the various elements which make up a film: the characters, the setting and the plot.
- Say what the film is about, giving the title, genre, name of the director and when it was made. Among other things, you may want to include awards and the names of actors.
- Give background information on the film and the director.
- Give specific information on what the film is about and provide a short summary without giving away the ending (unless this is explicitly required). You should aim to make your audience curious and encourage them to watch the film themselves rather than give everything away.
- Finish the review with your personal opinion (on the actors' performance or the adaptation of the novel, for instance), give reasons for your opinion and say whether you would recommend it or not.
- Remember to structure your review into three main parts:
  - an introduction with a catchy first sentence,
  - a main body outlining your main points (one per paragraph),
  - a conclusion summarizing the points made.

Useful vocabulary:

The film was produced/directed by ...
It is set in / covers a period of / tells the story of ...
The main characters are ...
The story is rather weak/boring/unconvincing.
The storyline is entertaining/gripping/fascinating/clever.
I can thoroughly recommend the film.

4 HOW TO ANALYSE FILM STILLS

When analysing a film still, concentrate on the following aspects:

- the content and setting of the still: what can be seen in the picture and where? When and where is the action set?

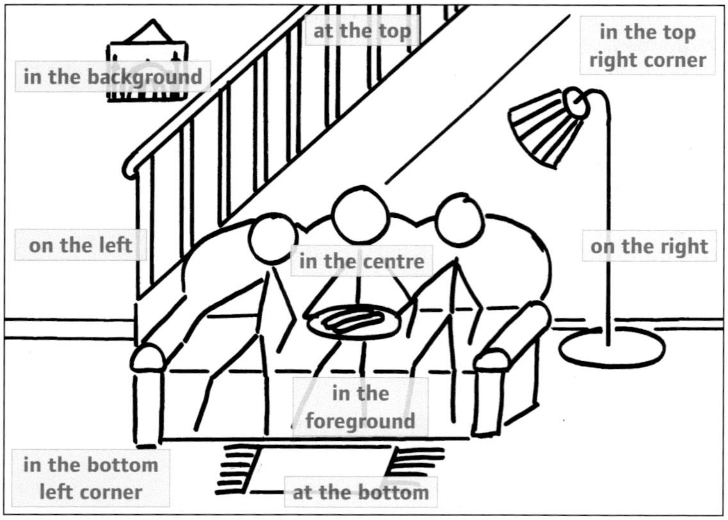

- the proportion of objects in the still; their arrangement in the foreground or background
- the camera angle and the perspective from which the still is taken
- the lighting and the colours of the still
- the overall impression: what impression is created by the above aspects?

Useful vocabulary:

The field size is a The camera takes a	long medium close …	shot	
The persons are The scene is …	filmed	from at	below above eye-level

1 Choose any still from the film and describe its major features to a partner. Make sure that your partner cannot see the original picture. Your partner draws a sketch while listening to your description. Then compare both pictures.